The Only Book You Will Ever Need for Money Management

By Daniel Melehi

©2023

Contents

4

Introduction

Welcome to *The Only Book You Will Ever Need for Money Management.*

In this comprehensive guide, we will explore the essential principles and strategies to help you effectively manage your finances and achieve your financial goals. Money management is a skill that is crucial for everyone, regardless of their income or financial situation. Whether you are just starting out on your financial journey or looking to improve your current financial well-being, this book has valuable insights and practical tips to offer. Financial management involves more than just budgeting and saving; it requires a holistic approach that encompasses various aspects of personal finance, such as investing, credit management, debt repayment, and retirement planning. By mastering these key areas, you can take control of your financial future and secure a stable and prosperous life. Throughout this book, we will take you on a step-by-step journey, providing you with the knowledge and tools to equip yourself with sound money management skills. From understanding the basics of money management to exploring advanced strategies for saving, investing, and planning for retirement, this book covers a wide range of topics to cater to your financial needs. To enhance your learning experience, each chapter is designed to be engaging and informative, presenting practical examples and real-life scenarios that you can relate to. We encourage you to actively participate in the exercises and reflect on your own financial circumstances as you progress through the book. Remember, knowledge is power, but action is what will truly transform your financial life. By the end of this book, we aim for you to have a solid foundation in money management and feel confident in making informed financial decisions. Our ultimate goal is to empower you to achieve financial freedom, allowing you to live the life you desire, free from financial stress and worry. So, let's embark on this journey together and delve into the world of money management. Whether you are a beginner or a seasoned financial enthusiast, there is something valuable for everyone within these pages. Get ready to take charge of your financial future and unlock a world of financial possibilities.

Chapter 1: The Basics of Money Management

Money management is a fundamental skill that everyone should possess. Whether you have just started earning an income or have been working for years, understanding the basics of money management is essential to achieve financial stability and success. In this chapter, we will explore the key principles and strategies that form the foundation of effective money management.

THE IMPORTANCE OF MONEY MANAGEMENT

Money management is not just for the wealthy or those with high incomes. It is a vital skill that anyone can develop, regardless of their financial situation. Properly managing your money allows you to make informed financial decisions, prioritize your expenses, and reach your financial goals. By practicing effective money management, you gain control over your finances and reduce the stress and anxiety that often accompany financial instability. It enables you to live within your means, avoid debt, and build a solid financial foundation for the future.

THE HOLISTIC APPROACH TO MONEY MANAGEMENT

Money management involves more than just budgeting and saving. It encompasses a holistic approach that includes various aspects of personal finance. These include budgeting, saving, investing, credit management, debt repayment, and retirement planning. Each of these areas plays a vital role in your overall financial well-being. Understanding how these different aspects of money management interconnect is crucial. For example, creating a budget helps you allocate your income effectively, which in turn allows you to save for the future, invest wisely, and manage your debt responsibly. It is crucial to have a comprehensive understanding of each component to make informed financial decisions.

BUILDING YOUR MONEY MANAGEMENT FOUNDATION

To build a strong money management foundation, it is important to start with a clear understanding of your current financial situation. This involves assessing your income, expenses, assets, and debts. By having a complete picture of your finances, you can create a solid foundation from which to build your financial goals and strategies. Once you have assessed your current financial situation, it is important to set realistic and achievable financial goals. Whether it is saving for a down payment on a house, paying off student loans, or building an emergency fund, having clear goals provides direction and motivation for your financial journey.

Key Takeaways

- Money management is an essential skill for everyone, regardless of income or financial situation. - It involves a holistic approach encompassing budgeting, saving, investing, credit management, debt repayment, and retirement planning. - Understanding and assessing your current financial situation is the first step in building a strong money management foundation. - Setting realistic and achievable financial goals provides direction and motivation for your journey towards financial stability. - By developing effective money management skills, you can gain control over your finances and work towards achieving financial freedom. In the next chapter, we will dive deeper into the process of setting financial goals and explore strategies to help you achieve them. Stay tuned as we continue on this journey towards mastering money management.

Chapter 2: Setting Financial Goals

Setting financial goals is a crucial step in the journey to achieving financial success and stability. Without clear goals, it becomes challenging to create a roadmap for your financial future. In this chapter, we will explore the importance of setting financial goals and provide practical tips on how to define and prioritize your objectives.

THE SIGNIFICANCE OF SETTING FINANCIAL GOALS

Gives Direction and Purpose

Setting financial goals gives you a clear direction and purpose for your money. It helps you identify what you truly want to achieve and provides motivation to take the necessary actions. Whether your goals include buying a house, starting a business, saving for retirement, or paying off debts, having specific targets allows you to focus your efforts and make informed financial decisions.

Provides a Framework for Decision-Making

When you have well-defined financial goals, it becomes easier to make decisions that align with your objectives. Every financial choice you make, from small daily expenses to major investments, can be evaluated based on how it contributes to your long-term goals. This framework helps you prioritize and allocate your resources effectively, ultimately leading to better financial outcomes.

Offers Measurement and Evaluation

Setting financial goals provides measurable benchmarks to track your progress. Your goals act as milestones that allow you to assess your financial health and determine if you are on track. Regularly reviewing and evaluating your progress against your goals helps you stay accountable and make adjustments as necessary.

Increases Financial Confidence

When you set financial goals and actively work towards achieving them, you gain a sense of control and confidence over your financial future. This confidence stems from knowing that you are making intentional decisions and taking steps towards your desired outcomes. As you accomplish your goals, your confidence in your ability to manage money effectively will grow.

STEPS TO SETTING FINANCIAL GOALS

1. Assess Your Current Financial Situation

Before setting financial goals, it is crucial to have a clear understanding of your current financial situation. Take a comprehensive look at your income, expenses, assets, and liabilities. Are you in debt? Do you have any savings? Are you living within your means? Understanding where you stand financially will help you set realistic goals that are attainable within your current circumstances.

2. Define Your Short-Term and Long-Term Goals

Next, identify your short-term and long-term goals. Short-term goals typically cover a period of one year or less and might include objectives like saving for a vacation or purchasing a new gadget. Long-term goals extend beyond five years and might include goals like saving for a down payment on a house or building a retirement fund. Make sure your goals are specific, measurable, achievable, relevant, and time-bound (SMART).

3. Prioritize Your Goals

Once you have identified your goals, prioritize them based on their importance and urgency. Start with the most critical goals that require immediate attention and work your way down. This will ensure that you allocate your time, energy, and resources effectively, maximizing your progress towards achieving your goals.

4. Break Down Goals into Actionable Steps

Breaking down your goals into smaller, actionable steps makes them more attainable and less overwhelming. Identify the specific actions you need to take to move closer to each goal. For example, if your goal is to save for a down payment on a house, your actionable steps might include creating a budget, cutting back on unnecessary expenses, and saving a specific amount each month.

5. Set Realistic and Achievable Targets

While it is essential to dream big, it is equally important to set goals that are realistic and achievable. Consider your financial resources, constraints, and timeframes when defining your targets. Setting overly ambitious goals can lead to frustration and discouragement if they are not realistic within your current circumstances.

6. Review and Adjust Your Goals Regularly

Financial goals are not set in stone. As your circumstances change, it is necessary to review and adjust your goals accordingly. Life events, economic fluctuations, and personal priorities may require you to reevaluate your objectives periodically. Regularly reviewing and adjusting your goals ensures that they remain relevant and responsive to your evolving financial circumstances.

CONCLUSION

Setting financial goals provides a roadmap for achieving financial success. By giving direction, providing a framework for decision-making, offering measurement and evaluation, and increasing financial confidence, these goals play a vital role in your financial journey. By following the steps outlined in this chapter, you will be empowered to set meaningful goals and take intentional actions towards making your financial dreams a reality. Remember, your financial goals are a reflection of your values and aspirations, so embrace the journey and enjoy the sense of empowerment that comes with taking control of your financial future.

Chapter 3: Creating and Sticking to a Budget

Managing your money effectively begins with creating a budget. A budget is a financial plan that outlines your income and expenses, providing a clear picture of your financial health and helping you achieve your financial goals. It enables you to make informed decisions about how you spend and save your hard-earned money.

THE IMPORTANCE OF BUDGETING

Creating and sticking to a budget is crucial for several reasons:

1. Financial Awareness

A budget allows you to understand your income, expenses, and spending patterns. It helps you identify areas where you may be overspending or not allocating enough funds. By tracking your spending, you can take control of your financial situation.

2. Goal Setting

A budget serves as a roadmap for achieving your financial goals. It helps you allocate funds to different areas, such as savings, debt repayment, and investments. With a clear plan in place, you can prioritize your financial objectives and work towards them.

3. Avoiding Debt

By creating a budget, you can prevent or reduce the accumulation of debt. It allows you to allocate funds for necessary expenses and save for emergencies, reducing the reliance on credit cards or loans to cover unexpected costs.

4. Saving for the Future

Budgeting enables you to set aside money for your future needs and aspirations. Whether it's saving for a down payment on a house, starting a business, or planning for retirement, a budget allocates funds to your savings goals and ensures disciplined saving habits.

STEPS TO CREATING A BUDGET

To create an effective budget, follow these steps:

1. Assess Your Income and Expenses

Start by gathering information on your income sources, including salaries, bonuses, side hustles, and investment returns. Next, track your expenses for a month, categorizing them into fixed expenses (rent/mortgage, utilities, healthcare) and variable expenses (groceries, dining out, entertainment).

2. Set Financial Goals

Determine your short-term and long-term financial goals. Whether it's paying off debt, saving for a vacation, or investing in your retirement, your goals will shape the allocation of your resources in the budget.

3. Prioritize Your Expenses

Decide which expenses are essential and which can be reduced or eliminated. Prioritize necessary expenses like rent, utilities, and groceries. Identify areas where you can cut back or find more cost-effective alternatives.

4. Allocate Funds

Divide your income into different categories, allocating specific amounts to each expense category. Ensure that your expenses do not exceed your income. Leave room for savings and unexpected expenses by creating an emergency fund category.

5. Track and Adjust

Implement your budget and track your spending regularly. Use budgeting tools or apps to monitor your progress and make adjustments as needed. Review your budget monthly or quarterly to ensure that it is aligned with your financial goals and current situation.

TIPS FOR STICKING TO YOUR BUDGET

Sticking to a budget can be challenging but is vital for financial success. Here are some tips to help you stay on track:

1. Be Realistic

Set realistic expectations when creating your budget. Don't be too strict or ambitious; allow some flexibility for unexpected expenses or occasional treats.

2. Use Envelopes or Digital Tools

Consider using the envelope system, where you allocate cash to different categories in labeled envelopes. Alternatively, use digital tools and apps that automatically categorize and track your spending.

3. Stay Disciplined

Develop the discipline to resist impulsive purchases and stick to your budget goals. Find ways to motivate yourself, such as visualizing your financial goals or rewarding yourself when you achieve milestones.

4. Review and Adjust Regularly

Regularly review your budget to ensure it remains aligned with your financial goals and circumstances. Adjust it as needed to accommodate changes in income, expenses, or financial goals.

5. Seek Accountability and Support

Find an accountability partner or join a budgeting support group to stay motivated and share experiences. Engaging with others who are on a similar financial journey can provide valuable insights and encouragement. By creating and sticking to a budget, you gain control over your financial life. It empowers you to make informed decisions about your money, work towards your financial goals, and ultimately achieve financial freedom. Start budgeting today and unlock the path to a more secure and prosperous future.

Chapter 4: Saving Strategies for Every Income Level

Saving money is essential for everyone, regardless of income level. It provides financial security, enables you to achieve goals, and gives you the freedom to live life on your terms. While saving may seem challenging, there are strategies that can be implemented at every income level to make it attainable and effective. In this chapter, we will explore different saving strategies designed to accommodate various income levels and help you build a strong financial foundation.

UNDERSTANDING YOUR CURRENT FINANCIAL SITUATION

Before diving into saving strategies, it's crucial to assess your current financial situation. Take stock of your income, expenses, debt, and any existing savings. Understanding where your money is coming from and where it's going will provide valuable insight into areas where you can cut costs and save more effectively.

STRATEGIES FOR LOW-INCOME EARNERS

If you are earning a low income, saving money may feel like an impossible task. However, with careful planning and commitment, it can be done. Here are some strategies specifically designed for low-income earners:

1. Prioritize Your Expenses

When money is tight, it's essential to prioritize your expenses. Focus on covering your basic needs, such as food, housing, and utilities, first. Look for ways to cut back on discretionary expenses, such as eating out or entertainment, and redirect those funds towards savings.

2. Automate Your Savings

Set up automatic transfers from your checking account to a separate savings account. Even if you can only save a small amount each month, automating the process ensures that it happens consistently and helps you build a savings habit.

3. Utilize Government Programs and Resources

Research and take advantage of government programs and resources available for low-income individuals. These programs may provide assistance with housing, healthcare, childcare, and other essential needs. By reducing these costs, you can free up more money for savings.

4. Look for Additional Sources of Income

Consider taking on a side gig or freelance work to supplement your income. Even a part-time job or small side business can provide extra funds that can be directed towards savings.

5. Embrace Frugal Living

Adopting a frugal lifestyle can make a significant difference in your ability to save. Look for ways to cut costs, such as shopping sales, buying in bulk, cooking at home, and limiting discretionary spending. Every small saving adds up over time.

STRATEGIES FOR MIDDLE-INCOME EARNERS

For those with a moderate income, saving can still pose challenges, but it is more attainable. Here are some strategies geared towards middle-income earners:

1. Establish an Emergency Fund

Start by building an emergency fund to cover unexpected expenses or financial emergencies. Aim to save at least three to six months' worth of living expenses in a separate savings account. This fund will serve as a safety net and prevent you from relying on credit in times of financial stress.

2. Budget for Saving

Make saving a priority in your budget. Allocate a set percentage of your income towards savings before allocating funds to discretionary expenses. Treat your savings contribution as a non-negotiable expense, just like your rent or mortgage payment.

3. Maintain a Healthy Debt-to-Income Ratio

Strive to keep your debt-to-income ratio within a manageable range. Avoid taking on excessive debt that could hinder your ability to save and invest. Prioritize paying off high-interest debts, such as credit cards, and consider refinancing loans to lower interest rates.

4. Continuously Increase Your Savings Rate

As your income grows, gradually increase your savings rate. Commit to saving a certain percentage of any salary increases or bonuses you receive. This will help you avoid lifestyle inflation and accelerate your savings growth.

5. Diversify Your Savings

Explore different savings vehicles, such as a high-yield savings account, certificates of deposit (CDs), or individual retirement accounts (IRAs). Diversifying your savings allows you to take advantage of different interest rates and investment options.

STRATEGIES FOR HIGH-INCOME EARNERS

While high-income earners may have more resources to save, they also face unique challenges such as increased lifestyle inflation and complex tax considerations. Here are some strategies tailored for high-income earners:

1. Maximize Tax-Advantaged Accounts

Take advantage of tax-advantaged retirement accounts, such as employer-sponsored 401(k) plans and individual retirement accounts (IRAs). Maximize your contributions to these accounts to reduce your taxable income and benefit from potential employer matches.

2. Invest in Tax-Efficient Funds

Consider investing in tax-efficient funds, such as index funds or exchange-traded funds (ETFs), which generate fewer taxable capital gains distributions. This can help minimize your tax liability and maximize your investment returns.

3. Utilize Professional Advice

Consult with a financial advisor who specializes in working with high-income individuals. They can help you navigate complex financial situations, optimize your investments, and develop a comprehensive wealth management plan.

4. Set Stretch Savings Goals

Challenge yourself to set ambitious savings goals and strive to achieve them. Higher-income earners have the potential to save a significant portion of their income. Setting stretch goals ensures you are making the most of your earning power.

5. Give Back and Make a Difference

Consider philanthropic endeavors as part of your financial plan. Giving back to causes you care about not only benefits others but also provides a sense of fulfillment and purpose. Explore charitable giving strategies that align with your values and long-term goals. By implementing these saving strategies based on your income level, you can take significant steps towards building a robust financial future. Remember, saving is a journey, and it's never too late to start. Make saving a priority, stay disciplined, and regularly assess and adjust your saving strategies as your income and financial situation evolve.

Chapter 5: The Power of Compound Interest

Compound interest is a powerful financial tool that can work in your favor when it comes to growing your wealth. It is the concept of earning interest on both the original amount of money invested or saved, known as the principal, and the accumulated interest from previous periods. Understanding how compound interest works and harnessing its power can have a significant impact on your financial future. This chapter will delve deeper into the concept of compound interest, its benefits, and how you can leverage it to achieve your financial goals.

WHAT IS COMPOUND INTEREST?

Compound interest is a process in which interest is calculated and added to the initial principal amount, creating a new, larger base for future interest calculations. This means that not only will you earn interest on the original investment or savings, but also on any interest that has been accumulated over time. The compounding effect becomes more significant over longer periods. As the interest is compounded, the interest earned in each period adds to the principal, and subsequent interest is calculated based on the new, higher amount. This creates a snowball effect, allowing your money to grow exponentially.

THE BENEFITS OF COMPOUND INTEREST

The power of compound interest lies in its ability to accelerate the growth of your money over time. By consistently reinvesting your earnings, you can harness the compounding effect to achieve your financial goals faster. Here are some key benefits of compound interest:

1. Increased Wealth Accumulation

Compound interest enables your money to work harder for you, generating additional income without any additional effort from your side. As interest is reinvested or compounded, the growth potential of your investments or savings increases significantly. Over time, even small incremental contributions can grow into substantial sums.

2. Time Advantage

One of the most significant advantages of compound interest is the time factor. The earlier you start saving or investing, the more time your money has to grow. By taking advantage of compound interest from a young age, you can leverage the power of time to build substantial wealth in the long run.

3. Retirement Savings Boost

Compound interest is particularly advantageous when it comes to retirement savings. By starting to save for retirement early and consistently contributing to your retirement accounts, you can benefit from the compounded growth over several decades. This can provide you with the financial security and freedom you desire during your golden years.

4. Debt Reduction

Compound interest is not limited to investments and savings alone. It can also work against you when it comes to debt. Credit card balances, loans, and other forms of debt also accrue compound interest over time, increasing the total amount owed if not paid off promptly. Being aware of the power of compound interest can motivate you to prioritize debt repayment and minimize the financial burden in the long run.

HOW TO LEVERAGE COMPOUND INTEREST

To make the most of compound interest, it's important to adopt certain strategies and habits. Here are some tips to leverage compound interest effectively:

1. Start Early

The key to maximizing the power of compound interest is to start investing or saving as early as possible. The more time your money has to grow, the greater the compounding effect will be. Even small amounts contributed regularly can make a significant difference over a long time horizon.

2. Be Consistent

Consistency is key when it comes to harnessing the power of compound interest. Make it a habit to save or invest consistently, whether it's a fixed amount per month or a percentage of your income. Automating your contributions can help ensure consistency and eliminate the temptation to skip contributions during challenging times.

3. Reinvest Earnings

Reinvesting your investment earnings or interest is crucial for taking full advantage of compound interest. Instead of withdrawing the returns, allow them to accumulate and compound over time. This will supercharge the growth of your investments or savings.

4. Diversify Your Investments

Diversification is a key principle of investing. By spreading your investments across different asset classes, such as stocks, bonds, and real estate, you can reduce risk while still benefiting from the power of compound interest. A diversified portfolio can help protect your wealth and enhance its growth potential.

CONCLUSION

Understanding and harnessing the power of compound interest can be a game-changer in achieving your financial goals. By starting early, being consistent, reinvesting earnings, and diversifying your investments, you can maximize the growth potential of your money and build a solid financial future. Compound interest has the power to transform your financial journey and pave the way for financial independence and abundance. It's time to harness its power and unlock the path to wealth accumulation.

Chapter 6: Understanding and Improving Your Credit Score

THE IMPORTANCE OF YOUR CREDIT SCORE

Your credit score is a three-digit number that represents your creditworthiness. It is a tool that lenders use to assess your creditworthiness and determine the interest rates, terms, and conditions of any loans or credit you may apply for. A good credit score can open doors to better financial opportunities, while a poor credit score can limit your options and increase your costs. Understanding your credit score is crucial, as it directly impacts your ability to secure loans or credit cards, rent an apartment, buy a car, or even get a job. It is essential to actively manage and improve your credit score to ensure financial stability and achieve your long-term financial goals.

How Your Credit Score is Calculated

Your credit score is calculated based on various factors, including: 1. Payment History: This is the most critical factor, accounting for approximately 35% of your credit score. Lenders want to see that you make payments on time and in full. Any missed payments, late payments, or defaults can significantly impact your credit score. 2. Credit Utilization: This factor accounts for about 30% of your credit score. It measures the amount of credit you have borrowed compared to the total credit available to you. It is generally recommended to keep your credit utilization ratio below 30% to maintain a good credit score. 3. Length of Credit History: This factor accounts for about 15% of your credit score. Lenders prefer to see a longer and positive credit history, as it demonstrates your ability to responsibly manage credit over time. 4. Credit Mix: This factor accounts for around 10% of your credit score. Having a mix of different types of credit, such as credit cards, loans, and mortgages, can positively impact your credit score, as it shows your ability to handle different financial obligations. 5. New Credit Applications: This factor accounts for approximately 10% of your credit score. Opening multiple new credit accounts within a short period can negatively impact your score, as it may be seen as a sign of financial instability or overextending yourself.

How to Improve Your Credit Score

Improving your credit score takes time and effort, but it is achievable with the right strategies. Here are some tips to help you improve your credit score: 1. Pay Your Bills on Time: Make sure to pay all of your bills, including credit card payments, loans, and utilities, on time. Late payments can harm your credit score, so set up reminders or automatic payments to ensure you stay on track. 2. Reduce Your Credit Card

Balances: Aim to keep your credit card balances low and pay them off in full each month. This helps lower your credit utilization ratio and demonstrates responsible credit management. 3. Limit New Credit Applications: Avoid applying for multiple new credit accounts unless necessary. Each new application can result in a hard inquiry on your credit report, which temporarily lowers your credit score. 4. Monitor Your Credit Report: Regularly review your credit report for any errors or discrepancies. If you find any inaccuracies, dispute them with the credit bureau to have them corrected. 5. Diversify Your Credit Mix: If you have only one type of credit account, such as only credit cards or only loans, consider diversifying your credit mix by adding different types of credit. This shows lenders that you can handle various financial obligations responsibly. 6. Keep Old Accounts Open: Closing old credit accounts may negatively impact your credit score, especially if they have a long and positive payment history. Keep these accounts active and in good standing to maintain a healthy credit score.

Building and Maintaining Good Credit Habits

Building and maintaining good credit habits is essential for long-term financial success. Here are some additional tips to help you establish and maintain a healthy credit score: 1. Budget Wisely: Creating and sticking to a budget helps ensure you have enough money to cover all your expenses, including debt payments. It allows you to manage your credit effectively and avoid overspending. 2. Limit Your Debt: Minimize your debt by only taking on what you can afford to repay comfortably. Avoid carrying high balances on your credit cards or accumulating excessive loans. 3. Maintain a Stable Employment History: A consistent employment history demonstrates stability and reliability to lenders. It can positively impact your creditworthiness and improve your credit score. 4. Avoid Maxing Out Credit Cards: It's best to keep your credit card balances well below the credit limit. Maxing out your credit cards can negatively affect your credit utilization ratio and lower your credit score. 5. Be Mindful of Joint Accounts: When opening joint accounts, remember that any negative activity or missed payments by the other account holder can impact your credit score as well. Choose your joint account partners wisely and communicate openly about shared financial responsibilities.

Conclusion

Understanding and improving your credit score is essential for overall financial health and success. By actively managing your credit and following the tips provided in this chapter, you can take control of your creditworthiness and set yourself up for a brighter financial future. Remember, building and maintaining good credit habits is an ongoing process, so be patient and persistent in your efforts to achieve a high credit score.

Chapter 7: Different Types of Investments

Investing is an essential part of money management and building long-term wealth. It involves putting your money into various assets with the expectation of earning a return or generating income over time. In this chapter, we will explore the different types of investments available and their characteristics to help you make informed investment decisions.

UNDERSTANDING STOCKS

Stocks, also known as equities, represent ownership in a company. When you buy stocks, you become a shareholder and have the potential to benefit from the company's growth and profitability. Investing in stocks can be lucrative, but it also carries some level of risk. Stock prices can fluctuate based on market conditions, company performance, and other factors.

BONDS AND FIXED-INCOME INVESTMENTS

Bonds are debt securities issued by governments, municipalities, or corporations. When you buy a bond, you are essentially lending money to the issuer in exchange for regular interest payments and the return of the principal amount at maturity. Bonds are generally considered less risky than stocks, as they offer a fixed income stream and have a predetermined repayment schedule.

MUTUAL FUNDS

Mutual funds pool money from multiple investors to invest in a diversified portfolio of stocks, bonds, or other assets. They are managed by professional fund managers who make investment decisions on behalf of the investors. Mutual funds offer diversification and professional management, making them suitable for beginners or investors who prefer a hands-off approach.

EXCHANGE-TRADED FUNDS (ETFS)

ETFs are similar to mutual funds but trade on stock exchanges like individual stocks. They provide exposure to a specific index, sector, or asset class. ETFs offer diversification, flexibility, and low costs compared to mutual funds. They can be bought and sold throughout the trading day at market prices, providing liquidity to investors.

REAL ESTATE INVESTMENTS

Real estate investments involve buying properties or investing in real estate investment trusts (REITs). Owning physical properties can provide rental income and potential appreciation over time. REITs, on the other hand, allow investors to invest in a portfolio of properties without the need for direct ownership. Real estate investments can provide income stability and diversification.

COMMODITIES

Commodities are basic goods or raw materials that are traded on exchanges. Examples include gold, silver, oil, natural gas, agricultural products, etc. Investing in commodities can act as a hedge against inflation and provide diversification in an investment portfolio. However, commodities can be volatile and require a good understanding of market dynamics.

ALTERNATIVE INVESTMENTS

Alternative investments include hedge funds, private equity, venture capital, art, collectibles, and more. These investments are considered non-traditional and have the potential for higher returns but also carry higher risk. Alternative investments are typically suitable for sophisticated investors with a higher risk tolerance and longer investment horizons.

RISK AND RETURN

Before investing, it's crucial to understand the concept of risk and return. Generally, investments with higher potential returns tend to carry higher levels of risk. It's essential to assess your risk tolerance, investment timeframe, and financial goals before allocating your money to different investment types.

DIVERSIFICATION AND ASSET ALLOCATION

Diversification is a strategy that involves spreading investments across different asset classes to reduce risk. Asset allocation refers to the distribution of investments in different asset classes, such as stocks, bonds, and cash. Both diversification and asset allocation are important for building a well-balanced portfolio that aligns with your risk tolerance and financial goals.

CONCLUSION

Understanding the different types of investments available is crucial for making informed decisions and building a well-rounded investment portfolio. Each investment type has its own characteristics, risks, and potential returns. It's essential to assess your risk tolerance, investment goals, and timeframe before choosing the right investment mix that aligns with your financial objectives. Remember, diversification and regular review of your portfolio are key to long-term investment success.

Chapter 8: Building an Emergency Fund

An emergency fund is a crucial component of a strong financial foundation. It serves as a safety net to protect you from unexpected expenses or income disruptions. Building an emergency fund requires discipline and planning, but the peace of mind it provides is well worth the effort.

WHY IS AN EMERGENCY FUND IMPORTANT?

Life is unpredictable, and unexpected expenses can arise at any time. From unforeseen medical bills to car repairs or sudden job loss, having an emergency fund can prevent these situations from derailing your financial stability. Here are a few reasons why building an emergency fund is important:

1. Financial Security

Having a well-funded emergency fund provides a sense of security and peace of mind. It allows you to handle unexpected expenses without resorting to high-interest credit cards or loans. Instead of feeling stressed about how to cover these costs, you can confidently rely on your emergency fund.

2. Avoiding Debt

Without an emergency fund, you may find yourself relying on credit cards or loans to cover unexpected expenses. This can lead to accumulating debt and paying high interest rates over time. Having an emergency fund allows you to avoid falling into debt traps and maintain control over your finances.

3. Flexibility and Independence

An emergency fund gives you the freedom to make choices without being solely dependent on your paycheck. It provides a financial cushion that allows you to explore new opportunities, take career risks, or handle unexpected life changes.

HOW MUCH SHOULD YOU SAVE IN AN EMERGENCY FUND?

The amount you should save in your emergency fund may vary depending on personal circumstances. However, as a general rule of thumb, aim to save at least three to six months' worth of living expenses. This should cover essential costs such as rent/mortgage, utilities, groceries, and debt payments. If you have dependents or face higher job instability, consider saving even more to ensure you are adequately protected in case of longer periods of unemployment or other unforeseen circumstances.

STRATEGIES FOR BUILDING AN EMERGENCY FUND

Building an emergency fund requires consistent effort and dedication. It may take some time to reach your goal, but following these strategies can help you build your fund efficiently:

1. Set a Monthly Savings Goal

Determine how much you can comfortably save each month and set a goal for your emergency fund. Break this down into manageable monthly increments to track your progress effectively. Make saving a priority and treat it as a non-negotiable expense, just like paying your bills.

2. Automate Your Savings

To make saving easier, automate your savings by setting up recurring transfers from your checking account to a separate savings account designated for your emergency fund. This way, the money is set aside before you have a chance to spend it.

3. Reduce Expenses and Increase Income

Look for ways to reduce your monthly expenses and redirect that money towards your emergency fund. Consider cutting back on non-essential purchases or finding ways to save on bills and subscriptions. Additionally, explore opportunities to increase your income through side hustles or negotiating a higher salary.

4. Save Windfalls and Bonuses

If you receive unexpected windfalls, such as tax refunds or work bonuses, resist the temptation to splurge. Instead, allocate a portion or the entirety of these unexpected funds towards your emergency fund. This can significantly accelerate your progress.

5. Keep Your Emergency Fund Separate

To avoid dipping into your emergency fund for non-emergency expenses, keep it separate from your regular checking or savings accounts. Consider opening a high-yield savings account or a money market account specifically for your emergency fund. This separation will help you resist the temptation to use the funds for non-essential expenses.

CONCLUSION

Building an emergency fund is a critical step towards financial security and peace of mind. It provides a safety net to protect you from unexpected expenses and income disruptions. By setting a savings goal, automating your savings, and reducing expenses, you can steadily build your emergency fund. Start today and take control of your financial future.

Chapter 9: Managing Debt and Loan Repayment Strategies

Debt is a common aspect of modern financial life, and managing it effectively is crucial for maintaining financial stability and achieving long-term financial goals. This chapter explores the different types of debt, strategies for managing debt, and effective loan repayment strategies.

UNDERSTANDING DIFFERENT TYPES OF DEBT

Not all debts are created equal, and understanding the different types of debt can help you prioritize your repayments more effectively. Here are some common types of debt: 1.

Secured Debt:

This type of debt is backed by collateral, such as a house or a car. Failure to repay the debt may result in the collateral being seized by the lender. 2.

Unsecured Debt:

Unsecured debt does not have any collateral attached to it. Credit cards and personal loans are examples of unsecured debt. Lenders rely on your creditworthiness to determine whether to grant you the loan. 3.

Student Loans:

Student loans are specifically used to finance education. They often come with favorable repayment terms and lower interest rates compared to other types of debt. 4.

Mortgages:

Mortgages are used to finance the purchase of a home. They typically have a long repayment period and lower interest rates compared to other loans. 5.

Auto Loans:

Auto loans are used to finance the purchase of a vehicle. The vehicle itself serves as collateral for the loan.

STRATEGIES FOR MANAGING DEBT

Managing debt effectively is crucial for maintaining financial stability and achieving your financial goals. Here are some strategies to consider: 1.

Create a Debt Repayment Plan:

Start by assessing all your outstanding debts, including the amounts owed, interest rates, and repayment terms. Prioritize your debts based on interest rates or the snowball or avalanche method. 2.

Consolidate Debt:

Debt consolidation involves combining multiple debts into a single loan. This can simplify repayment and potentially lower your interest rate. 3.

Negotiate with Creditors:

If you're struggling to repay your debts, consider reaching out to your creditors to negotiate more favorable terms, such as reduced interest rates or extended repayment periods. 4.

Seek Professional Assistance:

If you find it challenging to manage your debt on your own, consider reaching out to a credit counseling agency or a debt management company for professional assistance.

LOAN REPAYMENT STRATEGIES

Aside from managing your overall debt, it's essential to have a plan in place for repaying individual loans. Here are some strategies to consider: 1.

Pay more than the minimum:

Whenever possible, pay more than the minimum required payment. This will help you reduce your overall interest costs and pay off the loan sooner. 2.

Utilize the debt snowball method:

This method involves paying off your smallest debts first while making minimum payments on larger debts. As you pay off smaller debts, you gain momentum and motivation to tackle larger debts. 3.

Utilize the debt avalanche method:

This method involves paying off the debt with the highest interest rate first while making minimum payments on other debts. This strategy can save you more money on interest payments in the long run. 4.

Consider refinancing:

If you have high-interest loans, refinancing them to a lower interest rate can help you save money and pay off the loan faster.

CONCLUSION

Effectively managing debt and implementing smart loan repayment strategies is essential for achieving financial stability and maintaining a healthy financial future. By understanding the different types of debt, creating a debt repayment plan, and utilizing strategies like debt consolidation and negotiation, you can take control of your debt and work towards a debt-free future. Remember, paying off debt requires discipline and commitment, but the rewards of financial freedom and peace of mind are well worth the effort.

Chapter 10: Strategies for Increasing Your Income

In today's world, increasing your income is not only desirable but also essential for achieving financial stability and reaching your financial goals. Whether you want to pay off debt, save for a down payment on a house, or invest for retirement, having more money coming in can make a significant difference in your financial situation. In this chapter, we will explore several strategies that can help you boost your income and take control of your financial future.

1. EXPLORE SIDE HUSTLES AND FREELANCING OPPORTUNITIES

One of the most popular ways to increase your income is by taking on a side hustle or engaging in freelancing work. Thanks to technology, there are countless opportunities available both online and offline. You can consider leveraging your skills and expertise to offer services such as graphic design, writing, programming, consulting, or tutoring. Platforms like Upwork, Fiverr, and TaskRabbit can help connect you with clients who are looking for your specific skills. By dedicating a few hours each week to a side hustle, you can earn extra income to supplement your regular job.

2. ENHANCE YOUR SKILLS AND EDUCATION

Investing in your skills and education can open up new opportunities for career advancement and higher-paying jobs. Consider enrolling in relevant courses, pursuing certifications, or even earning an advanced degree in your field of interest. This will not only make you more marketable but also increase your earning potential. Take the time to research what skills are in demand in your industry and take steps to acquire those skills. Continuously learning and growing can significantly impact your career trajectory and income.

3. NEGOTIATE FOR A RAISE OR PROMOTION

If you have been with your current employer for a while and have consistently delivered outstanding results, it may be time to have a conversation about your compensation. Schedule a meeting with your supervisor or human resources department to discuss your accomplishments and the value you bring to the company. Research salary ranges for your position and present a well-prepared case for why you deserve a raise. Be confident, articulate, and ready to negotiate. Keep in mind that timing is crucial, so choose an opportune moment to discuss your compensation.

4. START A SMALL BUSINESS

If you have an entrepreneurial spirit, starting a small business can be an excellent way to increase your income. This venture could be based on a hobby or passion you have, or it could be a gap you see in the market. Starting a business requires careful planning, research, and dedication, but it can be incredibly rewarding financially. Take the time to write a business plan, understand your target market, and develop a marketing strategy. Whether you decide to open an online store, offer a service, or become a consultant, starting a small business can provide you with an additional stream of income.

5. INVEST IN INCOME-GENERATING ASSETS

Investing in income-generating assets such as stocks, real estate, or bonds can be an effective way to increase your income over time. While these investments may require an initial capital outlay, they have the potential to provide passive income and grow in value. Before investing, make sure to thoroughly research the asset class and understand the associated risks. It is also advisable to seek professional advice if you are new to investing. By diversifying your income sources through investments, you can create a steady stream of income that complements your primary source of earnings.

CONCLUSION

Increasing your income is a powerful way to take control of your financial future. By exploring side hustles, upgrading your skills, negotiating for a raise, starting a small business, or investing in income-generating assets, you can create additional streams of income and accelerate your journey towards financial freedom. Remember, increasing your income is not a quick fix, but rather a long-term strategy that requires dedication, perseverance, and continuous learning. Stay focused, be proactive, and embrace opportunities that come your way. With the right mindset and strategies, you can increase your income and achieve the financial success you desire.

Chapter 11: Developing a Long-Term Savings Plan

Saving money is an essential aspect of financial management, and developing a long-term savings plan is a key component of building a secure financial future. While short-term savings goals are important for addressing immediate needs and emergencies, a long-term savings plan focuses on larger financial objectives such as retirement, homeownership, or education expenses.

1. ASSESSING YOUR LONG-TERM FINANCIAL GOALS

Before developing a long-term savings plan, it's crucial to assess your financial goals. Consider what you want to achieve in the future and estimate the amount of money you will need to accomplish these goals. Examples of long-term financial goals may include:

a. Retirement

Planning for retirement is critical to ensure financial security in your later years. Determine the age at which you want to retire and calculate the income you will need to sustain your lifestyle during retirement.

b. Homeownership

If you aspire to own a home, estimate the down payment and monthly mortgage payments you will need to make this dream a reality. Consider factors such as the current housing market, interest rates, and your desired location.

c. Education expenses

If you or your children plan to pursue higher education, calculate the amount of money you will need to cover tuition, books, and other educational expenses. Take into account the duration of the educational program.

2. SETTING SAVINGS TARGETS

Once you have identified your long-term financial goals, setting savings targets is crucial. Break down each goal into smaller, manageable savings targets. Consider the time horizon for each goal and the amount of money you can realistically save within that timeframe.

3. CHOOSING APPROPRIATE SAVINGS VEHICLES

Different savings vehicles have distinct features and benefits. Consider your risk tolerance, investment knowledge, and long-term goals when choosing the appropriate savings vehicles for your long-term savings plan. Common options include:

a. Individual Retirement Accounts (IRAs)

IRAs offer tax advantages and are specifically designed for retirement savings. Traditional IRAs allow for tax-deductible contributions, while Roth IRAs offer tax-free withdrawals in retirement. Research and understand the contribution limits and eligibility criteria for each type of IRA.

b. Employer-sponsored retirement plans

Many employers offer retirement plans, such as 401(k)s or 403(b)s, which often include employer matching contributions. Take advantage of these plans and contribute as much as possible to maximize employer matches and benefit from tax advantages.

c. Investment accounts

Consider opening investment accounts that allow you to invest in stocks, bonds, mutual funds, or exchange-traded funds (ETFs). This allows you to potentially earn higher returns over the long term but carries higher investment risks.

d. High-yield savings accounts and certificates of deposit (CDs)

These accounts offer relatively higher interest rates compared to regular savings accounts. They provide a safe and low-risk option for long-term savings.

4. AUTOMATING YOUR SAVINGS

To ensure consistent savings contributions, automate your savings. Set up automatic transfers from your checking account to your designated long-term savings accounts. This eliminates the temptation to spend the money and ensures regular contributions toward your long-term goals.

5. MONITORING AND ADJUSTING YOUR PLAN

Regularly monitor the progress of your long-term savings plan and make adjustments as needed. Revisit your goals and savings targets periodically to ensure they align with your evolving financial situation and priorities. Consider consulting with a financial advisor to review your plan and make any necessary modifications.

CONCLUSION

Developing a long-term savings plan is crucial for achieving financial security and reaching your future financial goals. By assessing your goals, setting savings targets, choosing appropriate savings vehicles, automating your savings, and regularly monitoring your progress, you can build a solid foundation for your long-term financial success. Remember, consistency and discipline are key to maintaining a successful long-term savings plan.

Chapter 12: Navigating the World of Taxes

Taxes are a crucial aspect of financial management, and understanding how to navigate the world of taxes can greatly impact your financial well-being. This chapter will provide you with essential knowledge and strategies to effectively manage your taxes and optimize your financial situation.

THE IMPORTANCE OF UNDERSTANDING TAXES

Taxes are the main source of revenue for the government and fund essential public services such as healthcare, education, infrastructure, and defense. It is crucial to understand the tax system to ensure compliance and maximize your financial resources.

The Different Types of Taxes

There are several types of taxes, each serving a specific purpose. Some of the common types of taxes include: 1. Income Tax: This is the tax paid on your earnings from various sources such as employment, business profits, investments, and rental income. 2. Sales Tax: Sales tax is levied on the purchase of goods and services and varies depending on the jurisdiction. 3. Property Tax: Property tax is based on the value of real estate properties and is used to fund local government services and infrastructure. 4. Estate Tax: Estate tax is levied on the transfer of assets after a person's death and is based on the value of the estate. 5. Capital Gains Tax: Capital gains tax is applied to the profit made from selling an asset, such as stocks, real estate, or collectibles.

Filing Status and Tax Brackets

When filing your tax return, it is important to determine your filing status and understand the tax brackets. The filing status depends on your marital status, and the tax brackets determine the percentage of your income that is subject to tax. Some common filing statuses include: 1. Single: This status applies if you are unmarried, divorced, or legally separated. 2. Married Filing Jointly: This status applies if you are married and file a joint tax return with your spouse. It may provide certain tax benefits. 3. Married Filing Separately: This status applies if you are married but choose to file separate tax returns. 4. Head of Household: This status applies if you are unmarried, have dependents, and pay more than half of the household expenses. Understanding the tax brackets will help you determine the percentage of tax you owe on different portions of your income. Tax brackets are divided into income ranges, and each range is subject to a specific tax rate.

STRATEGIES FOR MAXIMIZING TAX BENEFITS

While taxes are unavoidable, there are strategies you can implement to minimize your tax liability and maximize your tax benefits. Here are some key strategies to consider:

1. Take Advantage of Tax Deductions

Tax deductions are expenses that you can subtract from your taxable income, reducing the amount of tax you owe. Common deductions include: - Mortgage interest - Student loan interest - Medical expenses - Charitable contributions - State and local taxes - Business expenses By keeping track of eligible expenses and itemizing your deductions, you can potentially reduce your taxable income and lower your overall tax bill.

2. Contribute to Retirement Accounts

Contributing to retirement accounts such as a 401(k) or Individual Retirement Account (IRA) provides you with both short-term and long-term tax benefits. Contributions to these accounts are often tax-deductible, reducing your taxable income in the year of contribution. Additionally, investment earnings within these accounts grow tax-deferred, meaning you won't pay taxes on them until you withdraw the funds in retirement when you may be in a lower tax bracket.

3. Utilize Tax-Advantaged Accounts

There are various tax-advantaged accounts available that offer specific tax benefits. Some examples include: - Health Savings Account (HSA): Contributions to an HSA are tax-deductible, and withdrawals are tax-free when used for qualified medical expenses. - Flexible Spending Account

(FSA): Contributions to an FSA are made with pre-tax dollars, reducing your taxable income. Funds can be used for eligible medical expenses. - Education Savings Accounts: Accounts such as 529 plans offer tax advantages for education-related expenses, including tax-free growth and withdrawals for qualified educational expenses.

4. Consider Tax-Loss Harvesting

Tax-loss harvesting is a strategy used to offset capital gains by selling investments that have declined in value. By realizing capital losses, you can reduce your taxable income and potentially reduce your overall tax liability. It is important to consult with a tax professional or financial advisor when implementing tax-loss harvesting to ensure you comply with tax laws and regulations.

CONCLUSION

Navigating the world of taxes is an integral part of effective money management. By understanding the different types of taxes, your filing status, and utilizing strategies to maximize tax benefits, you can minimize your tax liability and optimize your financial situation. Remember, it is always recommended to consult with a tax professional or financial advisor who can provide personalized guidance based on your specific circumstances. By actively managing your taxes, you can take control of your financial future and make informed decisions to achieve your long-term financial goals.

Chapter 13: Insurance and Risk Management

THE IMPORTANCE OF INSURANCE

Insurance plays a crucial role in managing financial risks and providing protection against unforeseen events. It offers peace of mind and a safety net when unexpected situations arise. Whether it's health, life, property, or disability insurance, having the right coverage can help mitigate potential financial losses.

By paying a premium, individuals and businesses transfer risk to an insurance company. In return, the insurer agrees to cover potential losses, providing financial compensation when needed. Insurance helps protect against the financial burden of medical bills, property damage, legal expenses, and loss of income.

Types of Insurance

There are various types of insurance that individuals and businesses should consider:

- **Health Insurance:** Health insurance provides coverage for medical expenses, including doctor visits, hospital stays, medication, and preventive care. It helps protect against the financial burden of healthcare costs.

- **Life Insurance:** Life insurance provides a payout to beneficiaries upon the death of the insured. It helps ensure financial security for loved ones and covers funeral expenses, outstanding debts, and future expenses.
- **Auto Insurance:** Auto insurance provides coverage in the event of accidents, damage, or theft of a vehicle. It protects against any financial liability for property damage or injuries caused by the insured's vehicle.
- **Homeowners/Renters Insurance:** Homeowners insurance protects against property damage or loss caused by fire, theft, natural disasters, or liability claims. Renters insurance provides coverage for personal belongings and liability in rental properties.
- **Disability Insurance:** Disability insurance provides income replacement in the event the insured becomes unable to work due to illness

or injury. It helps maintain financial stability during periods of disability.

- **Liability Insurance:** Liability insurance covers legal costs and damages in the event the insured is held responsible for injuries or damages to other people's property. It can protect individuals and businesses from significant financial losses.

ASSESSING INSURANCE NEEDS

It's essential to assess insurance needs based on individual circumstances and financial goals. Consider the following factors when determining the appropriate level of coverage:

1. Personal Circumstances

Assess your personal circumstances to determine the type and amount of insurance needed. Consider factors such as age, health condition, dependents, and financial obligations.

2. Asset Protection

Consider the value of your assets, including property, vehicles, investments, and savings. Adequate insurance coverage protects these assets from potential loss or damage.

3. Risk Tolerance

Assess your risk tolerance and evaluate the likelihood of specific events. Consider the potential financial impact of these events and determine the level of coverage needed to feel secure.

4. Cost-Benefit Analysis

Weigh the cost of insurance premiums against the potential benefits and financial protection provided. Compare quotes from different insurers and choose coverage that offers the best value for your needs.

RISK MANAGEMENT STRATEGIES

In addition to insurance, there are other strategies for managing and mitigating financial risks:

1. Emergency Fund

Building an emergency fund is essential for handling unexpected expenses. Having a financial cushion helps cover immediate needs without relying solely on insurance claims.

2. Risk Identification

Identify potential risks and take steps to prevent or minimize their impact. This could involve implementing safety measures, improving security, or making necessary repairs or upgrades.

3. Diversification

Diversify investments to spread risk across different asset classes. This helps reduce the impact of market volatility and provides a buffer against potential losses.

4. Regular Review and Updating

Regularly review insurance policies and coverage to ensure they align with changing circumstances and needs. Upgrading coverage or adjusting deductibles may be necessary as financial situations evolve.

5. Seek Professional Advice

Consult with insurance agents or financial advisors to understand personal insurance needs and make informed decisions. They can provide valuable guidance in selecting the right policies and coverage amounts.

CONCLUSION

Insurance and risk management are integral parts of a comprehensive financial plan. By understanding the importance of insurance, assessing individual insurance needs, and employing risk management strategies, individuals can safeguard their financial well-being and protect against potential financial hardships.

Remember, insurance provides a safety net, and sound risk management strategies offer added financial security. Taking proactive steps to manage and mitigate risks allows individuals to navigate unexpected events with greater confidence and peace of mind.

Chapter 14: Retirement Planning for a Secure Future

INTRODUCTION:

Retirement planning is an essential aspect of money management that ensures financial security and a comfortable lifestyle in the future. It involves setting long-term financial goals, saving diligently, and making smart investment decisions. In this chapter, we will explore the importance of retirement planning, strategies for building a substantial retirement nest egg, and the different retirement saving options available to individuals. By the end of this chapter, you will be equipped with the knowledge and tools to plan for a secure and enjoyable retirement.

WHY RETIREMENT PLANNING MATTERS:

Retirement is a phase in life when we no longer rely on active employment income, and our savings and investments become our primary source of financial support. Without careful planning and preparation, we risk facing financial difficulties or having to compromise our desired lifestyle during retirement. Retirement planning is crucial for several reasons: 1. Financial Security: Retirement planning ensures that you have enough funds to cover your living expenses and enjoy a comfortable lifestyle during your retirement years. 2. Inflation Protection: The cost of living tends to rise over time due to inflation. By planning for retirement, you can account for inflation and ensure that your savings keep pace with the increasing costs. 3. Longevity Risk: People are living longer than ever before, and retirement can last for several decades. Adequate retirement planning can help mitigate the risk of outliving your savings. 4. Independence and Flexibility: Retirement planning allows you to maintain financial independence and have the flexibility to pursue activities and experiences that bring you joy and fulfillment.

BUILDING YOUR RETIREMENT NEST EGG:

To build a substantial retirement nest egg, it is important to start saving early and consistently. Here are some strategies to consider: 1. Determine Your Retirement Goals: Start by estimating the lifestyle you envision during retirement. Consider your desired level of comfort, travel plans, hobbies, and healthcare needs. This will help you determine how much money you will need to save. 2. Calculate Your Retirement Savings Gap: Once you have an estimate of your retirement goals, calculate the difference between your projected savings and the amount you need to maintain your desired lifestyle. This will give you an idea of how much you need to save to bridge the gap. 3. Maximize Retirement Accounts: Take advantage of tax-advantaged retirement accounts such as 401(k)s, IRAs, and Roth IRAs. Contribute the maximum allowed amount each year, and if your employer offers a matching contribution, be sure to contribute enough to receive the maximum match. 4. Diversify Your Investments: Invest your retirement savings in a diverse range of assets such as stocks, bonds, and mutual funds. Diversification helps spread the risk and can potentially increase your returns over the long term. 5. Monitor and Adjust: Regularly review your retirement savings progress and make adjustments as necessary. Consider consulting with a financial advisor to ensure you are on track and to make any necessary changes to your investment strategy.

RETIREMENT SAVING OPTIONS:

There are various retirement saving options available to individuals, each with its own benefits and considerations. Here are some common options to consider: 1. Employer-sponsored Retirement Plans: Many employers offer retirement plans such as 401(k)s or 403(b)s. These plans often include employer matching contributions, making them an attractive option for retirement savings. 2. Individual Retirement Accounts (IRAs): IRAs are available to individuals and offer tax advantages. Traditional IRAs allow you to contribute pre-tax dollars, while Roth IRAs allow you to contribute after-tax dollars and offer tax-free withdrawals in retirement. 3. Social Security: Social Security provides a steady income stream during retirement, but it is important to supplement this with other retirement savings as it may not be enough to cover all living expenses. 4. Annuities: Annuities are insurance products that provide a guaranteed income stream in retirement. They can be a useful tool for creating a stable income source, but be sure to carefully evaluate the terms and understand the fees associated with annuities.

CONCLUSION:

Retirement planning is a crucial component of money management that ensures financial security and a comfortable lifestyle in your retirement years. By setting retirement goals, saving diligently, and making smart investment decisions, you can build a substantial retirement nest egg and enjoy the retirement you have always envisioned. Take the time to understand your retirement options and seek professional advice when needed. Start planning for your secure future today, and reap the rewards of a well-prepared retirement.

Chapter 15: Real Estate Investments and Homeownership

Real estate investments and homeownership play significant roles in building wealth and achieving financial stability. In this chapter, we will explore the benefits of real estate investments, the process of buying a home, and strategies for successful property ownership.

BENEFITS OF REAL ESTATE INVESTMENTS

Investing in real estate offers several advantages that can contribute to long-term financial success. Here are some key benefits: 1. **Appreciation:** Real estate has the potential to appreciate over time, allowing investors to earn a profit when they sell the property. 2. **Income Generation:** Rental properties can provide a steady stream of rental income, offering an additional source of cash flow. 3. **Tax Advantages:** Real estate investors can enjoy tax benefits, such as deducting mortgage interest, property taxes, and repairs from their taxable income. 4. **Diversification:** Investing in real estate diversifies your investment portfolio, reducing risk by spreading investments across different asset classes. 5. **Inflation Hedge:** Real estate tends to keep pace with inflation, preserving the value of your investment over time.

THE PROCESS OF BUYING A HOME

Buying a home is a significant financial decision that requires careful planning and consideration. Here are the key steps involved in the home buying process: 1. **Assess Your Financial Situation:** Determine how much you can afford by evaluating your income, expenses, savings, credit score, and debt-to-income ratio. 2. **Get Pre-Approved for a Mortgage:** Meet with a lender to determine the amount you qualify for and obtain a pre-approval letter. This will give you a clear budget while searching for homes. 3. **Find a Real Estate Agent:** Working with a professional real estate agent can help you navigate the home buying process, find suitable properties, and negotiate the best deal. 4. **Search for Homes:** Use online listings, attend open houses, and visit neighborhoods to find properties that meet your criteria. 5. **Make an Offer:** Submit a written offer to the seller, including contingencies, closing dates, and any additional terms or conditions. 6. **Negotiate and Complete Inspections:** Negotiate the terms of the purchase contract and complete inspections to assess the property's condition. 7. **Secure Financing:** Finalize your mortgage application, provide the necessary documentation, and coordinate with your lender to secure financing. 8. **Complete the**

Closing Process: Review the closing documents, sign legal agreements, pay closing costs, and transfer ownership of the property.

STRATEGIES FOR SUCCESSFUL PROPERTY OWNERSHIP

Once you become a homeowner, it is important to implement strategies for successful property ownership. Here are some tips to consider: 1. **Have an Emergency Fund:** Set aside funds specifically for home maintenance and unexpected expenses. 2. **Maintain the Property:** Regularly maintain and update your home to preserve its value and prevent costly repairs in the future. 3. **Monitor the Real Estate Market:** Stay informed about market trends to assess the value of your property and consider opportunities for future investments. 4. **Consider Renting:** If circumstances change, you may consider the option of renting out your property to generate additional income. 5. **Property**

Management: If managing your own property becomes overwhelming, hiring a property management company can alleviate the responsibilities associated with maintenance and tenant management. 6. **Review Financing Options:** Periodically assess your mortgage terms and explore refinancing options if interest rates drop or your financial situation changes. 7. **Reap the Benefits:** As your property appreciates in value, you may choose to sell it to reap the financial benefits or leverage it to acquire additional investments.

Conclusion

Real estate investments and homeownership provide opportunities for wealth creation and financial stability. By understanding the benefits of real estate investments, navigating the home buying process, and implementing strategies for successful property ownership, you can make informed decisions that contribute to long-term financial success. Remember to stay proactive, stay informed, and regularly review your real estate portfolio to ensure it aligns with your financial goals.

Chapter 16: Teaching Children and Teens about Money

Teaching children and teenagers about money is a vital step towards setting them up for financial success in the future. By instilling good money habits early on, we can empower the next generation to make wise financial decisions and build a solid foundation for their financial well-being.

THE IMPORTANCE OF FINANCIAL EDUCATION FOR CHILDREN AND TEENS

Financial education for children and teenagers is essential for several reasons: 1. Developing Money Management Skills: Teaching children about money from a young age helps them understand the value of money, differentiate between needs and wants, and develop budgeting and saving skills. 2. Forming Good Habits: By teaching children about money, we can guide them towards developing responsible spending habits, saving regularly, and distinguishing between long-term and short-term goals. 3. Building Financial Confidence: Financial education helps children and teenagers feel confident and empowered to manage their finances effectively, setting them up for future financial success. 4. Avoiding Future Debt: By teaching children about the risks and consequences of debt, they can understand the importance of borrowing responsibly and avoid falling into debt traps later in life.

STRATEGIES FOR TEACHING CHILDREN AND TEENS ABOUT MONEY

Teaching children and teenagers about money can be done in various creative and engaging ways. Here are some effective strategies:

1. Start Early:

Introduce the concept of money and its value from a young age. Teach them how to count and identify coins and bills. Encourage them to save money in piggy banks or clear jars, and involve them in simple financial decisions, like choosing between two snacks at the grocery store.

2. Make It Practical:

Create real-life scenarios to teach children about money management. Give them a small allowance and help them divide it into savings, spending, and giving categories. Encourage them to set savings goals and save for something they want.

3. Involve Them in Budgeting:

Invite your children to participate in family budgeting discussions. Explain the basics of budgeting, including income, expenses, and saving goals. Allow them to contribute their ideas and give them responsibility for specific budget categories, such as groceries or entertainment.

4. Teach the Value of Delayed Gratification:

Help children understand the concept of delayed gratification by teaching them to save for larger purchases. Encourage them to save a portion of their allowance or earnings for something they really want, rather than buying impulsively.

5. Teach Them About Earning:

Encourage children and teenagers to earn money through age-appropriate tasks or small jobs. This will help them understand the connection between work and money, and the importance of hard work and perseverance in achieving financial goals.

6. Discuss Saving and Investing:

Introduce the concepts of saving and investing to older children and teenagers. Teach them about the power of compound interest and the different types of investment options available. Help them open a savings account or start a small investment portfolio to learn hands-on about the potential for growth and earnings.

7. Encourage Giving and Philanthropy:

Teach children about the importance of giving back to the community and helping others. Encourage them to donate a portion of their money or time to a cause they care about. This fosters a sense of gratitude, empathy, and social responsibility.

8. Be a Role Model:

Children often learn best by observing their parents' actions. Model responsible financial habits by budgeting, saving, and making wise financial decisions. Discuss your financial choices with them, explaining the reasons behind them. This will help children understand the practical application of money management concepts.

CONCLUSION

Teaching children and teenagers about money is a crucial step in preparing them for a financially secure future. By starting early and using practical and engaging strategies, we can equip them with the knowledge and skills to make informed financial decisions. Remember to be a positive role model and actively involve children in financial discussions and activities. Together, we can empower the next generation to achieve financial well-being and success.

Chapter 17: Money-Saving Tips for Everyday Living

In this chapter, we will explore practical and effective money-saving tips that you can easily incorporate into your everyday life. These tips will help you stretch your budget, reduce unnecessary expenses, and save more money for your financial goals. By implementing these strategies, you will not only improve your financial situation but also develop a frugal mindset that will benefit you in the long run.

THE IMPORTANCE OF SAVING MONEY

Before we dive into the money-saving tips, let's briefly discuss why saving money is important. Saving money allows you to: 1. Build an emergency fund: Having savings set aside for unexpected expenses or financial emergencies will provide you with peace of mind and protect you from falling into debt. 2. Reach your financial goals: Whether it's buying a house, going on a dream vacation, or retiring comfortably, saving money is essential for achieving your long-term financial goals. 3. Create a safety net: Life is unpredictable, and having savings can help you navigate through tough times such as job loss or medical emergencies without relying on credit cards or loans. 4. Reduce financial stress: Knowing that you have money saved gives you a sense of security and reduces the stress that comes with living paycheck to paycheck.

MONEY-SAVING TIPS FOR EVERYDAY LIVING

Now, let's explore some practical strategies and tips to save money in your day-to-day life:

1. Create a budget:

Start by tracking your expenses and creating a monthly budget. This will help you identify areas where you can cut back and allocate your money towards your financial priorities.

2. Meal planning:

Plan your meals in advance and make a grocery list before going to the store. This will prevent impulse purchases and reduce food waste.

3. Cook at home:

Eating out can be expensive. Try to cook most of your meals at home, as it is not only cost-effective but also allows you to have control over the ingredients and portion sizes.

4. Use coupons and discounts:

Take advantage of coupons, promotional codes, and sales to save money on groceries, household items, and other purchases.

5. Reduce utility bills:

Save energy and reduce your utility bills by turning off lights and appliances when not in use, using energy-efficient light bulbs, and adjusting your thermostat.

6. Cut cable and streaming services:

Evaluate your cable and streaming subscriptions and consider cutting back or eliminating services you rarely use.

7. Cancel unnecessary subscriptions:

Review your subscriptions, such as magazines or subscription boxes, and cancel those you no longer find value in.

8. Comparison shop:

Before making a purchase, compare prices from different retailers to ensure you are getting the best deal.

9. Buy in bulk:

For items you frequently use, consider buying in bulk to take advantage of lower prices and save money in the long run.

10. Negotiate bills:

Don't be afraid to negotiate bills such as cable, internet, or insurance. Often, companies are willing to offer discounts or lower rates to retain customers.

11. Use public transportation or carpool:

If possible, opt for public transportation or carpooling to save money on gas and parking fees.

12. Minimize impulse purchases:

Take time to think about your purchases before making them. Avoid impulse buying and ask yourself if the purchase is truly necessary.

13. DIY instead of outsourcing:

Whenever possible, try doing things yourself instead of hiring professionals. Whether it's a simple home repair or a beauty treatment, learning new skills can save you money.

14. Embrace minimalism:

Simplify your life by decluttering and cutting back on unnecessary purchases. Focus on owning things that add value to your life and avoid unnecessary consumption.

15. Use cash instead of credit cards:

Paying with cash can help you become more aware of your spending and make it easier to stick to your budget.

16. Take advantage of free activities:

Look for free or low-cost activities in your community, such as local parks, libraries, or community events.

17. DIY gifts and cards:

Instead of buying expensive gifts or cards, consider making personalized DIY gifts or cards for special occasions.

18. Automate savings:

Set up automatic transfers from your checking account to your savings account to ensure consistent savings.

19. Shop second-hand:

Explore thrift stores, consignment shops, or online marketplaces for clothing, furniture, and other items. You can often find great deals on gently used items.

20. Practice delayed gratification:

Before making a purchase, give yourself a cooling-off period. If you still want the item after a few days or weeks, then consider buying it. Remember, saving money is a journey, and it requires discipline and commitment. Each small step you take towards implementing these money-saving tips will bring you closer to achieving your financial goals. By adopting a frugal lifestyle and making smart financial decisions, you can create a stable and prosperous future for yourself.

Chapter 18: Strategies for Saving on Groceries and Utilities

In this chapter, we will explore various strategies to help you save money on your groceries and utilities. These two expenses can often take up a significant portion of your budget, but with some smart planning and frugal habits, you can reduce your spending and keep more money in your pocket.

1. CREATE A MEAL PLAN AND STICK TO A SHOPPING LIST

One of the most effective ways to save money on groceries is by creating a meal plan and sticking to a shopping list. Before heading to the supermarket, take some time to plan your meals for the week. Consider the ingredients you already have and make a list of items you need to buy. Having a shopping list will prevent impulse buying and help you stay focused on purchasing only what you need.

Tip:

Try to base your meals on ingredients that are on sale or in season. This can help you save money and introduce some variety into your diet.

2. SHOP IN BULK AND TAKE ADVANTAGE OF SALES

Buying in bulk can be a great way to save money on groceries, especially for items that have a long shelf life. Look for sales and discounts on non-perishable items such as rice, pasta, canned goods, and toiletries. Buying these items in bulk can significantly lower your cost per unit.

Tip:

Consider joining a warehouse club, where you can find bulk quantities of groceries at discounted prices.

3. USE COUPONS AND CASHBACK APPS

Coupons can help you save money on groceries, so make sure to keep an eye out for them. You can find coupons in newspapers, magazines, online, and through mobile apps. Additionally, consider using cashback apps that offer rebates on your grocery purchases. These apps allow you to earn money back on specific products or receive cashback when you reach a certain spending threshold.

Tip:

Organize your coupons and use them when the items are on sale for even more savings.

4. REDUCE FOOD WASTE

Reducing food waste can save you money in the long run. Make sure to properly store and organize your food to prevent spoilage.

Additionally, consider meal prepping and freezing leftovers for future meals. By being mindful of what you have and using ingredients before they go bad, you can save money on groceries and minimize waste.

Tip:

Before grocery shopping, take a quick inventory of your pantry and refrigerator to avoid buying duplicates or items you already have.

5. CONSERVE ENERGY AND WATER

Saving on utilities is another important aspect of managing your finances. Implementing energy-saving habits can help reduce your electricity bill. Make it a habit to turn off lights when not in use, unplug electronics that are not being used, and use energy-efficient appliances. Additionally, conserve water by taking shorter showers, fixing leaks promptly, and using water-saving devices.

Tip:

Consider installing a programmable thermostat to regulate your home's temperature and optimize energy usage.

6. COMPARISON SHOP FOR UTILITIES

When it comes to utilities, such as electricity, gas, and internet services, it's essential to compare prices and plans. Don't be afraid to negotiate with service providers or switch to a different provider if it offers better rates. Doing your research and being proactive can lead to significant savings on your monthly utility bills.

Tip:

Consider bundling your services, such as internet and cable, to take advantage of discounted rates.

CONCLUSION

By implementing these strategies, you can save money on your groceries and utilities, freeing up more funds for other financial goals. Remember, small changes in your habits and planning can add up to significant savings over time. Stay diligent, track your spending, and continuously look for opportunities to cut costs and maximize your savings.

Chapter 19: Traveling on a Budget

Traveling is an enriching experience that allows us to explore new cultures, relax, and create lasting memories. However, it can also be expensive if not planned carefully. In this chapter, we will discuss strategies to travel on a budget without compromising on the quality of your experience.

BENEFITS OF TRAVELING ON A BUDGET

Traveling on a budget not only helps you save money, but it also allows you to have a more authentic and immersive experience. Here are some benefits of traveling on a budget: 1. Affordability: By consciously managing your travel expenses, you can save money that can be allocated for other financial goals. 2. Extended travel duration: Traveling on a budget allows you to extend your travel duration and spend more time exploring different destinations. 3. Immersion in local culture: When you travel on a budget, you are more likely to interact with locals, eat at local restaurants, and experience the true essence of the destination. 4. Unique experiences: By opting for budget-friendly options, you may discover hidden gems that are off the beaten path, providing a unique and memorable travel experience.

PLANNING YOUR TRIP

Proper planning is the key to a successful budget travel experience. Here are some steps to consider when planning your trip: 1. Choose affordable destinations: Research and select destinations that offer good value for money. Consider countries with a lower cost of living or off-peak travel seasons for cheaper accommodation and flights. 2. Set a travel budget: Determine how much you can realistically afford to spend on your trip. Take into account airfare, accommodation, meals, transportation, and activities. 3. Research accommodation options: Look for budget-friendly accommodation options such as hostels, guesthouses, or vacation rentals. Consider using websites and apps that offer discounted rates for accommodations. 4. Plan your itinerary wisely: Research free or low-cost attractions and activities in your destination. Prioritize the ones that interest you the most and fit within your budget.

SAVING ON TRANSPORTATION

Transportation costs can make a significant dent in your travel budget. Here are some tips to save on transportation: 1. Book flights strategically: Keep an eye out for flight deals and discounts. Be flexible with your travel dates and consider booking flights during off-peak seasons or midweek when prices tend to be lower. 2. Use alternative transportation options: Instead of solely relying on flights, consider other transportation options such as buses, trains, or carpooling services. These can often be more affordable, especially for shorter distances. 3. Walk or use public transportation: Explore the destination on foot or use public transportation whenever possible. This will not only save you money but also provide a more immersive experience.

EATING ON A BUDGET

Food can be one of the most significant expenses while traveling. Here are some strategies to save on meals: 1. Eat like a local: Opt for local street food or small family-owned restaurants to experience authentic cuisine at a lower cost. 2. Cook your own meals: If you have access to cooking facilities, consider buying groceries and cooking your own meals. This can be a cost-effective and healthier option for longer trips. 3. Pack snacks: Carry snacks with you to avoid impulse spending on expensive snacks or meals during the day.

ADDITIONAL TIPS FOR TRAVELING ON A BUDGET

Here are a few additional tips to help you make the most of your budget travel experience: 1. Travel during off-peak seasons: Prices for accommodation and flights are generally lower during off-peak seasons. Consider planning your trip accordingly to take advantage of these savings. 2. Use budget travel resources: Utilize budget travel websites, apps, and forums to find deals, discounts, and insider tips from fellow travelers. 3. Prioritize experiences over material items: Instead of spending money on souvenirs or material possessions, prioritize experiences and create lasting memories. 4. Be flexible and open-minded: Sometimes unexpected opportunities or last-minute deals can present themselves. Being flexible and open-minded allows you to take advantage of these opportunities and further stretch your budget.

CONCLUSION

Traveling on a budget doesn't mean sacrificing the quality of your experience. With careful planning, smart decision-making, and a willingness to embrace new experiences, you can enjoy memorable and fulfilling trips without breaking the bank.

By following the strategies outlined in this chapter, you can explore the world while keeping your finances in check. So, start planning your next budget adventure and embark on a journey of discovery and adventure!

Chapter 20: Staying Motivated and Maintaining Financial Discipline

The Importance of Staying Motivated

Maintaining financial discipline can be challenging, especially when faced with temptations or setbacks. However, staying motivated is essential for long-term financial success. Here are some reasons why staying motivated is crucial: 1. **Achieving Financial Goals:** Staying motivated keeps you focused on your financial goals. Whether it's saving for a down payment on a house, paying off debt, or building a retirement fund, staying motivated will help you stay on track and reach your goals faster. 2. **Overcoming Challenges:** Financial management often comes with unexpected challenges. By staying motivated, you'll be better equipped to handle these challenges and find creative solutions to overcome them. 3. **Building Financial Discipline:** Staying motivated helps you develop and maintain financial discipline. It allows you to stick to your budget, resist impulse purchases, and make wise financial decisions consistently. 4. **Creating Positive Habits:** Motivation plays a vital role in establishing positive financial habits. By staying motivated, you are more likely to develop habits such as saving regularly, tracking your expenses, and making informed financial choices.

Tips for Staying Motivated

Maintaining financial discipline requires continuous effort and dedication. Here are some tips to help you stay motivated: 1. **Set Clear and Realistic Goals:** Clearly define your financial goals and make sure they are realistic and achievable. Break them down into smaller milestones to stay motivated along the way. 2. **Reward Yourself:** Celebrate your accomplishments by rewarding yourself when you reach a financial milestone. This can be as simple as treating yourself to a small luxury or indulgence that aligns with your budget. 3. **Visualize Your Success:** Use visual reminders to keep your financial goals at the forefront of your mind. Create a vision board or use digital tools to visualize the life you want to achieve through your financial discipline. 4. **Track Your Progress:** Regularly track your progress to stay motivated. Use a budgeting app or spreadsheet to monitor your savings, debt repayments, or investment growth. Seeing your progress can reinforce your discipline and motivate you to keep going. 5. **Find an Accountability Partner:** Share your financial goals with a trusted friend or family member who can hold you accountable. Regular check-ins and discussions about your progress can help you stay on track and motivated. 6. **Stay Inspired:** Surround yourself with inspiration and positive financial resources. Follow personal finance blogs or listen to podcasts that share success stories, tips, and strategies. Learning from others can help you maintain motivation and learn new financial practices. 7. **Celebrate Small Wins:** Acknowledge and celebrate small financial wins along the way. Whether it's paying off a credit card or consistently saving a certain amount each month, recognize and appreciate the progress you are making. 8. **Stay Positive:** Maintain a positive mindset and believe in your ability to achieve financial success. Even when faced with setbacks, view them as opportunities for growth and learning rather than roadblocks.

Conclusion

Staying motivated and maintaining financial discipline is essential for achieving your financial goals and creating a secure future.

By understanding the importance of staying motivated, implementing the tips provided, and finding strategies that work for you, you can develop the discipline necessary to make wise financial decisions and build a stable financial future. Remember, financial discipline is a lifelong journey, and staying motivated will help you stay on track even during challenging times.